AN IDEAS INTO ACTION GUIDEBOOK

# Finding Your Balance

## IDEAS INTO ACTION GUIDEBOOKS

Aimed at managers and executives who are concerned with their own and others' development, each guidebook in this series gives specific advice on how to complete a developmental task or solve a leadership problem.

| | |
|---|---|
| LEAD CONTRIBUTORS | Joan Gurvis |
| | Gordon Patterson |
| CONTRIBUTOR | Patricia J. Ohlott |
| GUIDEBOOK ADVISORY GROUP | Victoria A. Guthrie |
| | Cynthia D. McCauley |
| | Ellen Van Velsor |
| DIRECTOR OF PUBLICATIONS | Martin Wilcox |
| EDITOR | Peter Scisco |
| ASSOCIATE EDITOR | Karen Mayworth |
| DESIGN AND LAYOUT | Joanne Ferguson |
| CONTRIBUTING ARTISTS | Laura J. Gibson |
| | Chris Wilson, 29 & Company |

CCL No. 427
ISBN No. 1-882197-87-9

CENTER FOR CREATIVE LEADERSHIP
POST OFFICE BOX 26300
GREENSBORO, NORTH CAROLINA 27438-6300
336-288-7210
WWW.CCL.ORG / PUBLICATIONS

AN IDEAS INTO ACTION GUIDEBOOK

# Finding Your Balance

Joan Gurvis and Gordon Patterson

Center for
Creative
Leadership

NORTH AMERICA EUROPE ASIA

www.ccl.org

## THE IDEAS INTO ACTION GUIDEBOOK SERIES

This series of guidebooks draws on the practical knowledge that the Center for Creative Leadership (CCL®) has generated in the course of more than thirty years of research and educational activity conducted in partnership with hundreds of thousands of managers and executives. Much of this knowledge is shared—in a way that is distinct from the typical university department, professional association, or consultancy. CCL is not simply a collection of individual experts, although the individual credentials of its staff are impressive; rather it is a community, with its members holding certain principles in common and working together to understand and generate practical responses to today's leadership and organizational challenges.

The purpose of the series is to provide managers with specific advice on how to complete a developmental task or solve a leadership challenge. In doing that, the series carries out CCL's mission to advance the understanding, practice, and development of leadership for the benefit of society worldwide. We think you will find the Ideas Into Action Guidebooks an important addition to your leadership toolkit.

# Table of Contents

## EXECUTIVE BRIEF

Balance isn't an issue of time, but an issue of choice. It's about living your values by aligning your behavior with what you believe is really important.

Aligning your behavior with your values is much like any other developmental experience; the basic process involves assessment, challenge, and support. You need to determine where you are, define where you want to go, and then put into place the tools you need to get there.

Balance is about more than how you spend your time. It's about how you live your life. It's about recognizing that you have control over the choices you make and aligning your behavior with your values.

# Balancing Act

People often define work-life balance as having equal or sufficient time for all they want to experience: career, family, friends, community, and leisure pursuits. Searching for the point of equilibrium or balance can become all-consuming and nonproductive.

But take a different look—one that says balance isn't an issue of time, but an issue of choice. You choose how to use your resources—what to do with your time, energy, and passion. Balance is more than an assessment of where and how you spend your time. It's about living your values by aligning your behavior—your choices and actions—with what you believe is really important.

A useful metaphor to keep in mind is a balance ball—the kind used for exercise and yoga. It looks as if it would be easy to sit on a balance ball, lift your feet off the floor, and balance your body. But the first few attempts are usually comical, if not disastrous. Success depends on a combination of purpose, practice, and patience. Eventually, you get a feeling of being centered. With attentive practice, you will be able to find your balance easily without having to think about your position or each move. It becomes a natural act.

Achieving balance or being centered in your life works in much the same way. Being in alignment or centered in life is about making clear choices that support your core values. The act of aligning your values and your life choices will achieve the same results as being centered on the balance ball. Doing so implies a dynamic process, just like sitting on the ball. You must constantly reassess your life, your challenges, and the consequences of your choices.

Values are the beliefs or feelings that are important enough to drive our decisions about how we behave. For one person, creativity, following a passion, and self-renewal can be major values. For another, knowledge, discovery, and intellectual curiosity can be drivers. For yet another, the attainment of material wealth, power, and status are key motivators of behavior. This is not to say that one is necessarily better than another; there are often no right or wrong answers, no absolutes. Our values shift during the course of our lives. Accordingly, so do the choices that flow from our different values. When our lives don't reflect the satisfaction of our values, we feel that inconsistency as some measure of imbalance.

Aligning your behavior with your values is much like any other developmental experience; the basic process involves assessment, challenge, and support. You need to determine where you are, define where you want to go, and then put into place the tools you need to get there.

Ann, a successful marketing manager, and her husband, Don, have two children under the age of five. Both Ann and Don are successful in their work, but Ann holds a senior position and earns significantly more than Don. They both travel a fair amount and rely on family and babysitters to help them. Each weekend, they sit down and plan their schedules for the week, determining who will run errands and pick up the children after preschool. Ann is grateful for Don's support. Things run smoothly most of the time, but she finds herself getting up before dawn to do e-mail and staying up late in the evening to finish household chores. She frequently admits that she misses spending quality time with her children. They could live on her salary alone, but they have recently purchased a vacation home and two new cars. With college and retirement ahead, neither Ann nor Don wants to live on one paycheck.

# Assessment: Gaining Clarity

Assessment helps you understand and gain clarity about your current situation so that you can identify the gaps between your present reality (where you are) and the future (where you want to be). Assessment provides you with information, which helps "unfreeze" your perspective, and results in a heightened awareness of yourself and understanding how others see you. A thorough assessment process becomes the "map" to help you move over the terrain and face the challenges that lie ahead. It is the process by which you develop new skills and perspectives that will help you become more effective in all aspects of your life.

## Time Journal

There are many ways to assess whether your values and behavior are aligned. One simple form of assessment is to inventory how you spend your time. Keep a log for a full week or two and jot down what you do for any period of time of an hour or more. Some themes or categories will emerge: career, family, community, health, self, spiritual pursuits, and so on. As a second step, write down why you did what you did. What value was being served? Next, consider the following questions:

- Are the activities in your log necessary for daily living, for your career, for your family, for your health, or simply for pleasure?
- What percentage of time did you spend in work-related activities versus family activities?
- How much time did you take for yourself?
- What inspires and rejuvenates you? Did you spend enough time on those activities?

# Warning Signs

We've listed below typical warning signs that we have learned about from our clients. Your life might be out of balance if . . .

1.  You have conversations with yourself in which you say, "I've got to make more time for my significant other." You hear yourself telling others that you really wish you had time to do certain things that you just don't get done now.

2.  Your relationships with your colleagues are less fun, less productive, and less easygoing than they used to be. From your point of view, your direct reports should be far more serious about work than they are. And you think that your family should appreciate you more than they do. They don't realize how hard you work for them.

3.  You are bone tired as well as frustrated, and you lean back to ask yourself why you stay at your computer long after the family has gone to bed. It's 2:37 a.m., and you can't recall exactly why you are sitting at your computer.

4.  The definitions of a perfectionist and type A personality that you read about years ago are descriptive of you. They have been descriptive of you for years. You now accept that you have not really even thought about altering your behavior. You realize that an appropriate place to start is by asking yourself why you are the way you are.

5.  You know you are good. You can multitask like there's no tomorrow. The speed of light is pretty fast. You know that you can run that fast for months on end. And people continually marvel at how you can "do it all." They think you are superhuman.

6. You pause mentally to put on your armor, to sharpen your lance, and to psych yourself up each day when you come through the front door of your office. You're so tired. You have to go through a dress rehearsal to get through each day.

7. You want to appear interested when your direct reports tell you about their newborn children, but you don't want them to conclude that their job responsibilities are any less important just because they've become parents. You feel that your own accomplishment will be called into question when they request favors and tell you that they will now have to spend time helping out at home.

---

- How much control or choice do you have about how you spend your time?
- What is beyond your control? Have these obligations, such as child care and elder care, changed over time?

As you review your journal, think about balance as you currently define it. Do you feel "in balance"? What does your assessment tell you? Put a check mark next to the activities that are not negotiable. Now consider the rest. Is the amount of time that you spend on each of the remaining activities in proportion to the others? Are there elements of tension or stress or instances where your interests create conflict and a sense of internal competition within yourself? For example, is your quest to be a better golfer driven by the desire to conduct more business or by the love of the game—or both? Or your interest in reading to learn more about your new personal computer so that you'll be able to do your own programming—does it conflict with a family value of being present at your child's weekend sports or scouting events? It's easy to confuse your interests with your values.

If there's been a gradual increase in your concern about balance, attempt to recall and make note of the critical incidents or insights that have accumulated for you. Finally, think about where your energy is focused. Is the amount of time you are spending on an activity related to the energy it requires? You may even decide to monitor the situation closely for a period of time to see whether other themes or trends emerge.

The choices you make about how you spend your time may well turn out to be consistent with what you value. On the other hand, the values you declare or profess may not be the ones you actually live. It's easy to *say* that you value something. Yet actually living by or following your values, actually *acting* on them, may be another matter entirely.

Knowing your current values and their priorities can help you attain more consistency between your values and your behavior. Consider the list of values on the next page. Circle the five values that you consider most important. Then go back and review your time journal. Do you see your values reflected in the way you spend your time? What is congruent? What is in conflict? What's missing?

## Other Views

An important part of the assessment process is seeking input and feedback from those around you. As a result of asking for feedback, you may realize that your intent—what you want to express—may not be visible to others. For example, your intent may be to come home on time and be with your family, when, in fact, your evening hours are consumed with paperwork and e-mail correspondence. What message are you really sending? Or perhaps your intent is to gain a promotion or be given a stretch assignment. But your boss notices only your constant criticism of the way

## Values

| | | |
|---|---|---|
| achieving goals | creativity | location |
| activity / action | earning high income | love |
| advancement / promotion | economic security | loyalty |
| adventure | enjoyment | order |
| aesthetics | fame | personal development |
| affiliation / belonging | family-like environment | physical fitness |
| authority | fellowship | recognition |
| autonomy | friendship | reflection |
| balance | happiness | responsibility |
| challenge | helping others | self-respect |
| change / variety | humor | spirituality |
| collaboration | influence / impact | status |
| competence | integrity | wisdom |
| competition | justice | |
| courage | knowledge | |

things are done now and doesn't see your desire to improve the processes.

Think about what the people who live or work closely with you might have to say about how you spend your time. Do you think that your values and priorities are being reflected in your relationships and interactions with them? Ask people you trust to tell you about their perceptions of you with respect to the values that they believe you are living by. Explain to them that your goal is to learn more about how others perceive your work-life balance. If a face-to-face conversation is not comfortable or possible, you could ask them to list things you should start, stop, and continue doing as they pertain to your relationship with them. It is wise to get both a personal and a professional perspective. What values would the members of your family attribute to you—if they could be completely candid with you? What values would they say you actually live, as opposed to the ones you espouse?

Once you have heard their feedback, think about what surprises you, disappoints you, and pleases you. What questions do you still have for them? Be careful to avoid the trap of trying to act upon the feedback immediately or to defend or justify your

> Paul is a single father. His wife passed away three years ago, leaving him with a teenage son. At the time, Paul was a senior investment broker at a wealth management firm, often working long hours and weekends. After his wife passed away, Paul left the firm, opting to start a financial planning business at home so that he could spend more time with his son. While his salary is significantly less than he earned as an investment broker, he enjoys the flexibility and freedom that his business offers him and wouldn't trade the time that he is able to spend with his son after school and in the evenings.

position. Just consider what you've heard and hold it lightly until you are clear about your next steps.

## Success

Your definition of success is a fundamental element of any assessment that you make about balance in your life. You undoubtedly devote a relatively significant amount of time and energy throughout your life to achieving whatever you have decided that success is. Your own definition of success drives your actions. It is your actions that are either in balance or out of balance.

For some of us, success can be a steadily increasing earnings level, higher levels of responsibility, status, prestige, and recognition in our careers. For others, it may be centered on family, community, self-actualization, or spiritual awareness. Many people seek some combination of rewards in both the personal and professional realms. Personal definitions of success can take many shapes and forms.

It is not uncommon for people to discover that they have never identified for themselves just how they define and measure success. What *really* drives you? What would be most difficult for you to let go of? Be honest with yourself. No one is looking. No one can read your mind. You will not have to tell anyone—unless you decide to.

The definition of success that you have today may not be at all like the one you held several years ago—or the one you will hold several years from now. Our concept of success is often formed in our homes when we are young. Are those early commandments and the expectations of others still relevant for you? If not, are you willing to free yourself from them?

Achieving success, for most of us, is not a solo endeavor. Others who are important to us may be wrestling with their own uncertainties about success at the very same time that we are. They may hope—or expect—that we will contribute to their sense of success. Frequently, we don't share with others our definitions of success. For that reason, they may well not understand why we devote time and energy to some things and not to others. It's not safe to assume that others define success the way we do or to try to impose our definitions on others. Their definitions of success may be completely different from ours. They may not see our success the way we do and might like to modify our definitions of success. As we reflect about success in our lives, we may find ourselves realizing that we are concerned about—perhaps even obsessed with—letting someone down. Our quest for success, as we have envisioned it, may be intended to please someone else.

# Challenge: Making Changes

Now that you have assessed where you are in your quest for a more balanced life and thought about where you would like to be, you are in a good position to determine the challenges you will face. Challenge is a necessary ingredient of a lasting developmental experience. Challenges seem to capture our attention first and more often than not consume most of our time and energy. We know we are challenged when we feel unable to cope, manage a situation, or find a solution to a problem we are facing. Habits and behaviors that were once effective no longer seem to work. Having the right amount of challenge prevents us from being bored and helps us to grow and learn, but when we are overly challenged, we are not able to adapt and cope as effectively.

The mere notion of enhancing balance in our lives and careers is, in itself, a daunting challenge. Just entertaining the possibility of

Paula is a fourth-grade teacher and graduate school student working on her master's degree in elementary education. One day, she hopes to become a school principal. In order to manage her work and course load, Paula gets up very early each morning to exercise before going to school. She finds that exercise gives her energy and helps her manage stress, and mornings are the only time she can schedule her workouts regularly. She has done volunteer work as a board member of a nonprofit organization, but she resigned recently in order to find more time for herself. She limits her use of social e-mail, choosing instead to call friends to stay in touch, and has joined a study group with others in her class for support and socialization.

examining our balance may be the very reason that we have yet to do anything about it. We are supremely conscious that doing something about the balance in our lives could be more of a challenge than we feel we can handle or even consider. We know that instinctively—even before we permit ourselves to focus our attention on the subject.

As we contemplate the challenge that might be before us, we are really evaluating the following:

- If I invest myself, what will I get in return?
- Just how much pain, frustration, anxiety, and lack of fulfillment do I feel?
- Am I really willing to start something without having any idea how it will turn out?
- Am I able to be totally honest with myself?

Choosing—and it is a deliberate, conscious choice—to devote more time and energy to pursuits that hold value for you and less time and energy to those that are less important can be extremely challenging. Sometimes the challenge emerges as a counterpoint to

# Facing Up

We've distilled below some common challenges that our clients have encountered as they tried to create more balance in their lives.

1.  You may have to take fewer red-eye flights. As a consequence, you will have fewer opportunities to impress your boss and colleagues with your high level of commitment by making sure that they know you flew all night the previous night— and that you are in the office the next morning before starting time.

2.  You may have to inform your significant other that you are becoming increasingly uneasy about the demands of the job because they're having a negative impact on your value about the importance of family. You may have to explain to your family that your income may suffer.

3.  You may have to bring your concerns about balance to your supervisor even though you have no idea what the reaction will be.

4.  Over the past few years you've been told by your last three bosses that you're performing very well and that you have a great deal of promise. You have celebrated quietly to yourself because of that praise. You're not certain what that means, especially now that you and your spouse have started a family. Perhaps you and your spouse will have to reevaluate your assumptions about what providing a nourishing family environment means.

5.  You are now aware that over the years, you've followed the advice of the human resources recruiter who lured you from

the college campus several years ago. The hard work, long hours, and effort you've devoted to accomplishing your objectives seem not to have resulted in your having what you expected. You may have to identify what you need to do differently.

6.  You've done your own evaluation of people who get promoted in your organization, but you have yet to discern a pattern that suggests to you that there are common threads of accomplishment and contribution. You realize that you need to find out what gets rewarded in your organization.

7.  You're concerned about telling—you won't be able to *ask*— your boss that you can no longer stay in the office so late on most evenings. Your spouse has grown extremely resentful of your not being home to help. Almost as difficult for you is the fact that your mother somehow managed so much when she was your age. And she had two more children than you do.

your view of balance itself. For example, a career disappointment or a personal hardship can force you to a sudden realization that at some level your life feels out of balance. A crisis can reveal a disconnect between your assumptions and your experience, triggering a need in you to redefine what you think is important. At other times, the challenge is related to the change you must make in order to gain your balance. This can be especially true in the workplace. Three common challenges to making personal changes are time, supervisory behavior, and fear.

## Time

People often say that managing time is more important than managing money. But what happens to our priorities when we have more to do than we can possibly accomplish in the time we have? What happens is that the time and energy that we devote to work often draws on family and personal time. Unless you take steps to protect time for your family and yourself, work usually encroaches.

Further, current technology makes us more accessible after hours and while traveling. Instant messaging, e-mail, voice mail, cell phones, laptops, personal digital assistants, pagers, and other devices can tether us to the office 24-7, blurring the line between work and family time. A rise in the number of people working from home blurs the boundaries even further.

Organizations are just beginning to recognize this as a serious concern for workers. We know that when retention issues are cited in the workplace as being problematic, balance issues frequently emerge as root causes.

## Supervisory Behavior

Some organizations do a better job of talking about balance than actually encouraging or providing for it. In some cases, it is difficult to get data from colleagues; they may not feel safe to talk freely with others about what they are contemplating. Your best barometer may be your perceptions of the levels of supervision above you and not what the policy manual seems to say. Even in an organization with supportive policies concerning work-life balance, the way you experience that support depends largely upon your boss. Immediate supervisors usually have the single most influential role in an organization when it comes to communicating organizational values and expectations, and deciding how policies will be implemented. Values related to balance may not be explicit or obvious, leaving them open to individual interpretation. Supportive managers will be flexible and understanding about your need to strike a different balance.

Ben and Elizabeth, both pharmaceutical sales managers, were married recently. They work in a large Midwestern city and cannot afford to live downtown, so they opted for a townhouse in the suburbs. Both have a ninety-minute commute each way. They drive separately because of different work schedules and frequently arrive home late. Dinners often consist of a quick bite on the go or take-out food from a neighborhood restaurant. Ben plays basketball in a city league and has games on weekends and many evenings. Elizabeth enjoys tennis and plays in an indoor league. Lately, they've noticed that they have little time together and find themselves leaving notes on the refrigerator to communicate. They agree that this is not what they want as newlyweds, but they are reluctant to cut back on their active lifestyle. They recently talked about finding something they could do together, such as golf or running.

Having open and frank conversations with your supervisor about your values and their relationship to your work is important in setting the tone for expectations and mutual understanding. Before accepting a new assignment or position, be aware of the value that is resonating within you. Is it material success, prestige, flexibility, challenge? Getting clear on that first may help you in making the best decision for yourself, your family, and your organization. Setting boundaries is an important and visible way to communicate clearly to others how you intend to lead your life. Be as explicit as you can about your reasons for time-related decisions to avoid misinterpretation. For example, if you have committed to leaving in time for dinner with your family and an emergency arises at work, how you manage the conflict will matter to both sides.

## Fear

Fear plays an important part in whether or not people will feel free to speak up about issues of balance in the workplace. The process of speaking up is influenced to a large degree by factors at the individual, group, and organizational levels. An environment that allows for and supports such dialogue between employee, supervisor, and peers is critical to understanding issues of balance in an organization. Fear of not being seen as a serious player or as someone who does whatever it takes and anxiety about being labeled as less dedicated are often underestimated and ignored as confounding factors.

# Support: Seeking Assistance

Another necessary ingredient of a lasting developmental experience is support. You don't have to do it all alone. You can reach out for support from others, or you can identify resources available to you and access them. It takes a conscious and deliberate effort to seek and accept support. In fact, it's your choice whether to ask for help. Many people tend to overestimate the amount of support in their lives and underestimate the challenge. So how can you balance these two elements?

## Honesty

Asking for help is not easy. We may have been led to believe that asking for help is tantamount to admitting failure. Our vulnerabilities immediately become obvious, or at least we feel that they do. Leaders who successfully balance competing demands in all aspects of their lives freely admit their vulnerabilities and frequently are admired and respected for doing so. It makes them seem more human and more approachable. Recognizing that you

Kent, who has achieved the rank of flag officer in the U.S. Navy, is reflecting upon his career and the ways in which he has accepted his responsibilities as an officer. His father led a distinguished military career. Kent realizes that he has modeled himself on his image of his father's values: duty, accountability, discipline, dependability, hard work, and sacrificing family life for extended periods. His seeing action in Vietnam hardened him in some profound ways. Kent now realizes that the assumptions about the "good life well lived" that he visited upon his son grew from what he learned from his father. Kent realizes that he has never decided for himself what he actually values in his own life. He hopes to be able to forgive himself for what he has taught his son and fervently longs for the day when his son will tell him that he loves him.

can't do it all is the first step in being honest about your strengths and developmental edges.

## Awareness of Limits

How often have you set a goal only to run into a wall—an obstacle that you felt was insurmountable? Human nature urges you to push harder and continue to focus on the same goal or behavior. What happens is that overused strengths often become liabilities; they don't get you where they used to. While it may seem counterintuitive to stop, ease back, or even shift focus, that's exactly what will get you unstuck. It's similar to working late at the office—fourteen hours a day, day in and day out. You are tricked into thinking that your efficiency is being maximized by your intense work efforts, when, in fact,

leaving early a few nights a week or delegating more is the solution. Know how hard you can push and when to step back and regroup. Others usually recognize these tendencies in us before we do, so being in a supportive environment is key to awareness.

# Where to Turn

We've listed below some possible sources of support as you consider the balance in your life.

1. You can describe your uncertainties to your parents. Seek their perspectives now that they are older and have lived through their own difficulties with having careers and providing a nourishing home environment for their children at the same time.

2. Confide your anxieties to a trusted mentor. Simply describing your problem out loud can bring a measure of reality to your thinking. Hearing yourself could even bring about a resolution or a decision about a course of action. Select at least one respected confidant of each gender.

3. Often there are differing or conflicting assumptions about gender roles in a relationship. It's not unusual for people to unconsciously adopt the gender roles played by their parents. You may not have even examined your own assumptions, much less articulated them. Consider sharing your respective assumptions in a dialogue with your partner. But be prepared. Deeply held convictions and assumptions can release very strong feelings.

4. Increasingly, men are staying at home to raise young children. Do income, self-concept, and career-planning strategies permit you to consider such an arrangement? Many support groups have sprung up for stay-at-home dads.

5. A trusted and respected colleague who appears to be in similar circumstances can provide an understanding ear as well as offer assurance that things are going reasonably well.

6. Your supervisor can be a source of information about your employer's work policies, both formal and informal. It is important to have a clear understanding of both your supervisor's and the organization's stance on the issue of balance. Your supervisor may even have concerns that are similar to yours.

7. Articles about balance are appearing more frequently. The *Wall Street Journal, Harvard Business Review,* and *New York Times* are among the mainstream periodicals that provide articles of opinion and research about balance.

## Recharging

Our capacity to work is not boundless, although we sometimes appear to believe otherwise. Our challenges fuel and drive this belief because they never seem to go away. Having enough support in our lives helps us to pursue the pleasurable activities that may have fled our souls—whatever they may be. Building in enough time to relax and recharge as we work is critical.

It is likely that almost everyone of a certain age is a veteran of the balance campaign. And if that's true, it follows that

• Your dealing with balance issues is not at all unique.

• You probably know numerous people who would be glad to draw upon their experience in order to lend a hand. Perhaps they could offer reassurance, suggest perspectives and actions they found useful, or at least know how to listen—having been there themselves.

• Those whom you turn to for support may well realize that you are seeking their input because you care about and respect them. They may even feel honored.

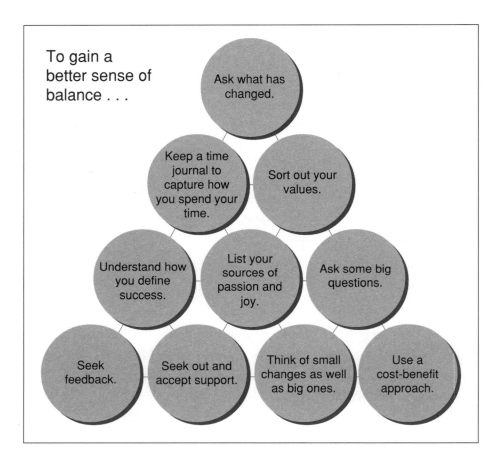

To gain a better sense of balance . . .

- Ask what has changed.
- Keep a time journal to capture how you spend your time.
- Sort out your values.
- Understand how you define success.
- List your sources of passion and joy.
- Ask some big questions.
- Seek feedback.
- Seek out and accept support.
- Think of small changes as well as big ones.
- Use a cost-benefit approach.

# Reality Sets In

Life events that all of us will inherit—and could not in any way anticipate—will call forth our best coping skills. Coping with unforeseen circumstances can require that we expend unusual amounts of care, concern, time, and energy. Some of these circumstances may invade other areas of our lives and become elements that we will balance in the future. When those circumstances

Dawn has always worked hard, starting many years ago when she was in school. She received numerous awards at graduation: scholastic, citizenship, character. Her scholastic and extracurricular record during her undergraduate years resulted in her early acceptance into one of the top M.B.A. schools. Now, after languishing in her career for the last nine years, she's decided to devote *more* time to her job and to formally declare her willingness to travel as much as necessary. Deep down inside, Dawn wants to make her mother proud of her. Dawn is certain that her mother could have been far more than a stay-at-home housewife. Dawn doesn't know how her husband of fourteen years will react. In fact, she's wondering whether she should tell him her intentions or simply wait to see what happens—and deal with his reaction when the time comes. She has decided not to mention her feelings about her mother.

occur, it will be both natural and inevitable to find ourselves agonizing about balance. With the passage of time, we may accept that we have survived—even thrived—and that our lives are flowing again. We may realize that balance was, in fact, never imperiled but that we temporarily made a choice to place one aspect of our lives ahead of another, knowing that things would eventually return to "normal" and that our equilibrium would be restored.

It is important to understand the context in which you'll deliberate as you consider how to begin to set some balance goals. Your circumstances may not be as serious as you imagine them to be, so a decision to do nothing, for whatever reason, may be a viable alternative. Your needs and expectations of yourself may have changed and will go on changing. In fact, the changes you make may not yield the results you hope for, especially at first, and they may bring unanticipated positive consequences. Remember that there is

> ### Leadership in the Balance
> What messages and expectations, some of them not so subtle, are you sending to those you lead—at the office and at home? You can be a very powerful role model for others without saying a word. What messages about balance do you send to your direct reports? What are your own children learning about balance in their lives as a consequence of observing you? Is it okay if your direct reports or your children or others who are important to you choose not to follow your lead—not to achieve as you have achieved, succeed by the same standards by which you have succeeded, gain the respect or prestige you have gained, find the meaning you have found? We are not the first, nor the last, generation to be concerned about balance—whatever each of us means by balance.

no fully appropriate, good, correct, satisfying balance for you (or anyone else). Embrace the presence of creative tension in your life—it can be a balance of sorts. No one promised you balance anyway! Only you are capable of making and implementing decisions that will be appropriate for you. It will be very easy—and tantalizingly tempting—to fix blame for your situation on persons and institutions you believe are responsible for your being out of balance.

Realize that working with your issues of balance may result in your feeling silly, vulnerable, and even out of control. If you alter your behavior, it's possible that others won't even notice that you have changed; you may not receive any kind of recognition or appreciation. But you can be proud of yourself if you do make some changes; you will have taken the initiative on something that's very important. You can also be proud of yourself if you accept, as a consequence of an honest inquiry into yourself, that you should not or cannot make changes at this time.

The important thing to remember is that balance is about more than how we spend our time. It's about how we live our lives. It's about aligning our behavior with our values.

# Suggested Readings

Friedman, S. D., & Greenhaus, J. H. (2000). *Work and family—allies or enemies? What happens when business professionals confront life choices.* New York: Oxford University Press.

*Harvard Business Review on work and life balance.* (2000). Boston: Harvard Business School Press.

Hochschild, A. R. (1997). *The time bind: When work becomes home and home becomes work.* New York: Metropolitan Books.

Kaplan, R. E. (with Drath, W. H., & Kofodimos, J. R.). (1991). *Beyond ambition: How driven managers can lead better and live better.* San Francisco: Jossey-Bass.

Kofodimos, J. R. (1993). *Balancing act: How managers can integrate successful careers and fulfilling personal lives.* San Francisco: Jossey-Bass.

Kofodimos, J. R. (1995). *Beyond work-family programs: Confronting and resolving the underlying causes of work-personal life conflict.* Greensboro, NC: Center for Creative Leadership.

Kofodimos, J. R. (1989). *Why executives lose their balance.* Greensboro, NC: Center for Creative Leadership.

Quick, J. C., Cooper, C. L., Quick, J. D., & Gavin, J. H. (2002). *The Financial Times guide to executive health: Building your strengths, managing your risks.* New York: FT Prentice Hall.

Ruderman, M. N., & Ohlott, P. J. (2000). *Learning from life: Turning life's lessons into leadership experience.* Greensboro, NC: Center for Creative Leadership.

# Background

This guidebook relies on a long trail of CCL research, dating back to the early 1980s and investigating how character shapes the way executives handle the relationship between their work and personal lives and how personal crises affect the way they restructure their lives. It also draws on CCL's work with executives in its Leadership Development Program, many of whom feel perplexed, concerned, and besieged by conflicting pressures at work and at home. As participants establish formal goals at the conclusion of the program, they are encouraged to consider balance in the professional, family, community, and personal aspects of their lives. Interestingly enough, work-life balance is rated by participants—before the program—as the least important area for development (twelfth out of twelve possible development areas from which participants select). After the program, participants rate work-life balance as the third most important focus for development, after improving self-awareness and self-confidence. Participants also frequently express concerns about balance during their private one-on-one meetings and feedback sessions with CCL coaches.

# Key Point Summary

Balance isn't an issue of time, but an issue of choice. It's about living your values by aligning your behavior with what you believe is really important. When your life doesn't reflect the satisfaction of your values, you feel that inconsistency as some measure of imbalance.

Aligning your behavior with your values is much like any other developmental experience; the basic process involves assessment, challenge, and support. You need to determine where you are, define where you want to go, and then put into place the tools you need to get there.

Assessment helps you understand and gain clarity about your current situation so that you can identify the gaps between your present reality and the future you desire. One simple form of assessment is to inventory how you spend your time. You can also seek input and feedback from those around you. Your definition of success is another fundamental element of your assessment.

When you have assessed where you are in your quest for a more balanced life, you will be in a good position to determine the challenges you will face. Three common challenges to making personal changes are time, supervisory behavior, and fear.

Another necessary ingredient of a lasting developmental experience is support. Recognize that you can't do it all. Know how hard you can push and when to step back and regroup. Your capacity to work is not boundless; building in enough time to relax and recharge is critical.

Balance is about more than how you spend your time. It's about how you live your life. It's about aligning your behavior with your values.

# Ordering Information

FOR MORE INFORMATION, TO ORDER OTHER IDEAS INTO ACTION GUIDEBOOKS, OR TO FIND OUT ABOUT BULK-ORDER DISCOUNTS, PLEASE CONTACT US BY PHONE AT 336-545-2810 OR VISIT OUR ONLINE BOOKSTORE AT WWW.CCL.ORG/GUIDEBOOKS. PREPAYMENT IS REQUIRED FOR ALL ORDERS UNDER $100.